MANAGE to SUCCESS

A Guide to Cultivating Happy and Productive Employees

LEISA REID

Founder, Employee Management Consulting

Editor: Jessica J. Hollowell
Cover Design: Fiona Jayde, *www.FionaJadeMedia.com*
Interior Design: Tamara Cribley, *www.DeliberatePage.com*

Library of Congress Control Number: 2016906860
CreateSpace Independent Publishing Platform, North Charleston, SC

Reid, Leisa

ISBN-13: 978-1530967070

ISBN-10: 1530967074

First Edition
    1. Business / Management
    2. Business / Communication
    3. Business / Personal Success
    4. Business / Mentoring and Coaching
    5. Business / Personnel Management

This book is available at quantity discounts for bulk purchases. For information, please visit *www.EmployeeManagementConsulting.com*

DEDICATION

This book is dedicated to my family. To my husband, Mark, the love of my life. To my daughter, Ariana, for whom I strive to be an example she can follow. To my mother, Jessica, for always cheering me on and for her teamwork and the knowledge she contributed to make this book a success. To my father, Bud, for his continued inspiration from the other side.

Finally, this book is dedicated to past employees and mentors who were my inspiration.

ACKNOWLEDGEMENTS

Until I wrote my own book, I never truly appreciated all of the people it takes to get it published. It really is a village! I'd like to acknowledge the following people for being a part of the *Manage to Success* village:

To my editor, Jessica J. Hollowell, who happens to be both my mom and an editor for over 30 years! We worked together so easily, sending drafts back and forth and back and forth and back and forth. It was fun to work with you on this project, and I appreciate all of your efforts and persistence. I will forever keep my dashes, ellipses, all capitals, exclamation points, parentheses and snarky comments to a minimum... (maybe).

To Tamara Cribley, my Interior Designer, I am so grateful to have you on my team.

To Fiona Jayde, my Cover Designer, you know your stuff! We worked together and you listened and asked excellent questions guiding me every step of the way.

To Adam Alexander, my Technical Genius, what you can do amazes me. Your gift of understanding all things technical is incredibly valuable. Every writer should have an Adam Alexander.

To Laura Lyon, you are there to listen and encourage me every step of the way as I get the knowledge in my head to the marketplace. I appreciate all of the time you have given me.

To my beloved OC Speakers Network, *www.ocSpeakersNetwork.com*. From our network I was inspired by and led to many people who supported this book. It is really cool to have almost all of your friends also be authors!

To Debbie Allen, none of this would have been possible without your challenge and direction. I am so grateful for your guidance and all that I have achieved and learned because of your expertise.

To Ursula Mentjes, my inspiration and favorite Sales Coach in Minnesota! You played an instrumental part in where I am today, including teaching Sales Camp, sharing the stage together, introducing me to Debbie and being an incredible author and leader.

To Leonard Szymczak and the writer's group: Laura Aiello, Stephanie Paul, Cassie Crow, Dr. Jeanne Michelle and Kat Tiley. Leonard, meeting you was a God send! Your enthusiasm is contagious. I am in deep appreciation for the connections you shared, advice you gave and all of the gold stars of encouragement.

To Jill Lublin, your generosity and knowledge are endless. I thank you for pointing me in the right direction, connecting me with other industry experts and being a strong support.

To the Productive Learning Staff, you are my other family and I wouldn't be where I am today without the incredible work you put into the world. To Andy, Warren, Lindon Austin, Lindon Oscar, Mark, Betty Jo and Cassie, thank you for all of your support, challenges and encouragement for me to live an extraordinary life.

I'd like to give a special thanks to three mentors. To Kerry Sousse who took a chance on me and hired me on the spot. To Valerie Curry who fought to hire me and took me under her wing. And, to Cassie Crow, who always wanted me and still tells me so.

A big shout out goes to my staff from AUOC. It was all of you who inspired me to share my management expertise with the world. Thank you for the memories, the hard work, the happiness and the productivity.

And to my family, Mark and Ariana. You both support me as I go from project to project and let me do my thing. Thank you for believing in me and allowing me to be free. I love you both more than words can say.

RAVE REVIEWS

"Leisa Reid knocked it out of the park with her book, *Manage to Success*. This is a great resource full of tools, tips and tactics on hiring and keeping employees that will save managers countless hours and headaches. It's a MUST READ for any manager!"

– **Debbie Allen**, Bestselling Author of *The Highly Paid Expert*
www.DebbieAllen.com

"*Manage to Success* is a required read for anyone who is promoted into management. The strategies and systems in Leisa's book will guide any manager through the challenges that they will face and help them save time and money in the long run. I wish I would have had this book when I was first promoted into management!"

– **Ursula Mentjes**, Award-Winning and Best-Selling Author of
Selling with Intention

"*Manage to Success* is a goldmine for managers looking to increase the productivity of their employees!"

– **Jill Lublin**, International Speaker and 3x Best Selling Author,
www.JillLublin.com

"Every manager needs this amazing book! In *Manage to Success,* Leisa Reid provides the essential tools and strategies in an easy-to-follow format for anyone responsible for hiring, training, and retaining staff. If you want practical tips to empower and motivate employees, improve communication and save time and money, buy this book!"

– **Leonard Szymczak**, Author of
The Roadmap Home: Your GPS to Inner Peace,
www.RoadMapHome.com

Contents

HOW IT ALL STARTED

My dad used to tell a story about sending me to day care. He specifically sent me to a Spanish speaking day care so I could become bilingual. However, when he picked me up, I had all the kids speaking English! I believe that was the birth of my management career.

Back in the early '90s, when I was officially paid to be a manager, I built a team of salespeople and *had absolutely no idea what I was doing.* I survived on pure luck and gumption. As my career developed and flourished over the years, I was fortunate to have excellent mentors to guide me. The information I am sharing with you in this book comprises the shortcuts and systems I wish I had known way back when.

Manage to Success includes many of the valuable lessons I've learned over the 20-plus years of my management career. This book was designed with the intention of saving you loads of time, money, and stress. Over my career, I have owned a business and worked for large national corporations and small family owned education institutes. By the time I was 22 years old, I was an instructor at California State University, Fullerton. By 27, I was a Director of Education for a college. At 30, I opened my own business, and by 36, I had sold that business and returned to the corporate world on my way to Executive Leadership. I learned many lessons along the way and want to share them so you, too, can be a successful leader.

Today I am a Speaker, Author, Consultant, and Trainer who works with thousands of people throughout Southern California each year. I founded Employee Management Consulting when I realized I could provide other managers with profitable solutions that dramatically reduce costly employee turnover.

My mission is to help create a healthier workplace for you and your staff, a place where everyone is both happy and productive. The goal is to make a workplace where managers and their employees can feel accomplished in their careers and be treated with kindness and respect. My goal is not to increase job satisfaction, but to create job elation.

For best results when reading through the book, take notes as you go through each chapter. By the time you complete the book, you will have several systems that you can easily implement.

Be prepared to have more time on your hands after you read *Manage to Success* and put the valuable systems in place that you are about to learn.

To Your Management Success,

Leisa Reid, M.A.
Speaker, Author, Consultant, Trainer
www.EmployeeManagementConsulting.com

Chapter 1

THE FIRST DATE

NAVIGATING THE INTERVIEW: Interviewing can make or break your success as a manager. Hiring is probably the most important part of your job, because the wrong person can cost you a significant amount of time and money. It is easy to get sidetracked and hire based on your initial impression of a jobseeker. This chapter offers *4 Interview Strategies* that will lead you to success in the interview process.

1. Be Consistent During Interviews
2. Pay Attention to Clues
3. Listen to Your Own Excuses
4. Focus on Valuable Long-Term Traits

Interview Strategy #1
Be Consistent During Interviews

Having a consistent interviewing system sets a baseline for you. It keeps you from getting wooed and charmed by your potential new hire. Consistency streamlines the decision-making process and helps you determine who will be the best fit.

You might think, "Well, I just like to interview people casually and have a natural conversation. I'm going to use my gut instinct to decide whether I want to hire this person."

Unfortunately, this method can be a big no-no.

That is not to say trusting your gut instinct doesn't play a part, but you may not always have a good instinct when it comes to hiring. Why? Because when applicants are interviewing, especially on their first meeting with you, they are on their very best behavior. They may have taken a job interview class and learned to prepare their answers and questions so flawlessly that you could be very easily fooled. They may be expert interviewees, but that is not what you care about.

What you care about is whether they are going to be excellent employees and a good match for your department and company.

What would a consistent interview process look like?

- *First*, during the weeding out process, go through the resumes with the same criteria for each position.
- *Second*, pre-screen all candidates with the same set of questions.
- *Third*, use the same questions in every face-to-face interview for that position.
- And *last*, have the same follow-up interview process for each person you are considering.

For this to work, you will need a specific list of questions that match the positions you are filling. Here are some guidelines to get you started.

Interview Question Guideline

- Ask open ended questions:
  - Tell me about ...
  - Give me an example of ...
  - Describe your last position ...
- Describe a specific time when you:
  - Worked with a team.
  - Went above and beyond.
  - Exceeded your goals.

- Ask for examples based on your needs for the position. For instance, if the position requires "attention to detail" then ask for a specific time in their past position(s) that they were detail-oriented.
- Find out their timeline for starting work at your company.
  - Tell them when you are looking to fill the position.
  - Ask if they are applying elsewhere.
  - Ask when they would be available to start.

Naturally, this doesn't mean you are supposed to sound like a robot and never deviate from your set of questions. Instead, you'll develop a consistent baseline that helps make your hiring decisions clear. You may ask various follow-up questions, depending on how the interview evolves, but you will also have a solid basis of comparison if it comes down to choosing between two great candidates.

Remember, the person with the most charming personality may not always be the best person for the job.

Interview Strategy #2
Pay Attention to Clues

I don't know about you, but I sure have gotten charmed during an interview. The person is so nice, friendly, bubbly, and witty. All of the above, right? And you are just beaming because you think, "Yay! I've found THE ONE; no more interviewing!"

Stop and get hold of yourself before making that job offer.

I'm NOT saying, by any means, that charming is necessarily a negative trait. It is a fantastic trait—if it's authentic, and if it helps employees do their job productively. What I am saying is that it's easy to be fooled by short-term, inauthentic charm in an interview situation. So what can you do when you feel yourself falling for the charmer sitting across from you?

This is where conducting a consistent interview will really pay off. Revisit the questions that you have developed for that position. By being consistent, you will be able to detect when the job candidate may be faking it. When you create your interview questions, ask for actual examples from their life or work history. When it comes to real examples, that charming person can maintain the false charm for only so long. Eventually, the charmer's real personality and choices will be revealed. But as the interviewer, you are like a detective. And you will need to pay attention to the clues they give.

Let's say you are hiring for a sales position. You may say:

> *"Please describe the goals of your last sales position and how you performed compared with the rest of the sales reps."*

Most high-performing sales people will remember their goals in detail, such as their daily quota and how to hit it. They also will know exactly how they performed in comparison to the rest of the team. Why? Because they typically have a competitive streak and like to be first. The best sales reps are focused on their goal and are passionate about hitting it every time. The way in which your interviewee answers this question will be very telling.

Clue 1: Are The Answers Vague?

- "It's hard to pinpoint what the exact goals were, but I always achieved them."
- "The goals were really high and I always hit them, but I can't recall any specifics."

Clue 2: Is Everything Someone Else's Fault?

- "The company was undergoing management changes, and it was a crazy time."
- "The past manager (a.k.a. the future you) gave the best leads to her favorites."
- "The company didn't give us solid leads, but I know that if I had good leads I could produce great results."

Think of these historical questions as a B.S. monitor. You want your questions to prompt actual examples of situations they have been in that relate to the job for which you are recruiting. If they cannot give you specific examples, they may have gotten through by their charm in the past. This is not to say that you cannot take a flyer on someone based on personality, knowing that you will be training him or her from the ground up. That can be a choice you make, but it also can be riskier than hiring someone with proven experience.

As you start to become consistent in your interviews and are looking intently for clues, you are going to want to turn up the volume on your inner voice.

Interview Strategy #3
Listen to Your Own Excuses

This strategy is a biggie, because it is really about you paying attention to you. There is a voice inside your head that makes excuses or urges you to settle because you are so busy and you really need that position filled yesterday. It is tempting. It is seductive. It is a mistake.

When you start to make any excuse for this future hire: Stop. Give yourself a timeout. Write down your excuse and run it by a trusted colleague. When you can see the excuse in writing or tell someone this excuse you are about to buy—literally, buy, because you'll be paying this person's salary—the correct decision will become obvious.

You want to think that you are making the best decisions, and it is tough to be honest about past hiring mistakes. But it's essential. Ask yourself, "Do I have an employee right now that I find myself making excuses for?"

Here are some possible scenarios.

Chris the Charmer
Chris is late for her first interview. Once she finally arrives, the interview is A-plus across the board. You really like her. She seems like a great fit, but she was late. OK, her excuse seems believable. Yes, traffic can be a problem. Your inner voice is screaming, "Hire her right now!"

Instead, stop, think it through and buy yourself some time. If Chris is a potential amazing employee, schedule a follow-up interview. If she returns for a second or even a third time, note her punctuality. If lateness is a deal breaker for you, drop her like a hot potato.

What if you just couldn't resist, and Chris is now on your team? Two weeks later, don't be shocked if she's already been late three times. And she always has a good excuse.

Problem Pat

In your interview filled with historical questions, you find out that Pat has a history of conflicts in the workplace. But, wow, her sales background is extremely impressive. She is really what you need right now to get the team's numbers up.

Do you hear yourself?

"So she had a couple of arguments with her co-workers who were stealing her leads. She closed the sale, and that's what really matters."

"Her other co-workers didn't include her in anything because they were jealous of her success. If she was as good as she says she is, I can see why they would be jealous."

Ask yourself these questions before you hire her:

Can I afford conflict on my team?

Do I have the time or skills to train her to resolve conflicts in a more effective way?

*In two months will the rest of the staff be lined up at my
door telling me they hate working with her?*

Remember, job candidates are supposedly on their very best behavior in the interview process. You need to know when to see through their B.S. and when to recognize the potential repercussions if you don't. These clues cannot be ignored.

Sadly, if you ignore them now, they will most definitely show up in the future. If you don't listen to the excuses you make now and end up settling, you, your team and, likely, your company will pay the price later.

Interview Strategy #4
Focus on Valuable Long-Term Traits

Two decades of management experience allowed me to see many personality traits. The 5 Traits listed below are ones that proved to be very valuable in terms of finding and keeping happy and productive employees:

- Consistency
- Reliability
- Going the Extra Mile
- Taking Responsibility
- Tolerance

As you read through these traits see which ones resonate for you, and then add your own to the list to keep in mind when you are interviewing.

Trait #1:
Consistency—A superstar one day and the bottom of pile the next, up-down-up-down, hard-working or slacking off. There is power and money in consistency, especially if you're consistently doing activities that are effective. In business and life, there are many

inconsistencies, but when you bring consistency into your activities day after day, you will see positive results.

> *The Pain of Inconsistency*—Karen, is the inconsistent employee. One week she is making things happen, she's in the zone, her customers are happy and her goals are being met. The next week, she is taking really long breaks. In fact, where did she go? Her results have flat-lined, and you are left wondering, "What went wrong?" You look at Karen's call logs and activities and see a big drop. What's the deal? Your head starts hurting.

> *The Consistent Employee*—Susie, the consistent employee, is the one who comes in each day at the same time, has a solid routine, completes the activities you have trained her to complete, and needs little direct supervision. The results are not all over the board, but consistent, because they match the activities Susie has put into her routine. Ah, you can sleep tonight.

If you find you have an inconsistent employee on your hands, you need to have a sit-down talk to share specific examples of when she has demonstrated inconsistencies and why you are concerned. She may not even be aware of what she is doing, so your first step is to shed the light and let her know what your expectations are moving forward.

Give her clear, easy steps to shift and show you that she can be consistent. Luckily, if this employee is providing value in other ways and you want to keep her and groom her, this is a coachable trait. Give her the chance to step up by sharing your observations and giving her clear guidance. If she refuses to take your guidance or is unable to change, then you can determine if she is someone you want to keep or not.

What kind of consistency do you want to see? Simply, the activities, attitude, and results that are in alignment with the goals of your department and the company.

Trait #2:

Reliability—You may have a superstar employee, but without reliability, expect major headaches. There is certain security and comfort knowing that you can rely on your staff, because reliability isn't just being there on time, it's much more! Does the team member actually do what she says she's going to do? Do the projected results become real? When she says she'll take care of something for you, does it get done?

> *The Pain of Unreliability*—Paula is often unreliable. You are never quite sure you are going to get the report you need when you need it. She is frequently too wrapped up in her personal drama to do her job. You walk to her desk and she's gone. No one knows where. Or she's at her desk, but you catch her posting on Facebook.

> *The Reliable Employee*—Marcella is the employee you can count on to do what she said she'd do. In fact, she sometimes anticipates what you'll need next. She arrives on time every day and spends her time at work producing results. If you delegate something to Marcella, not only will she do it in the proper time frame, it'll be done well.

During the hiring process ask the prospective employee for examples of when they were reliable in their past position(s). Have them give you a specific example.

If you find yourself with an unreliable employee, share your expectations and let her know you are looking for her to demonstrate reliability. If you find her to be a valuable employee in other areas, but this is an area of development, give her some coaching and energy. If you can see that this is just one of her many poor qualities, you can begin to document the conversations you have and possibly develop a case for termination.

Trait #3:

Go the Extra Mile—This is one of my favorite traits in an employee. When I was a kid, my Dad told me that wherever you worked, you should always leave it better than when you got there. When I actually started working, I quickly realized that not everyone has the same philosophy.

> *The Pain of Not Going the Extra Mile*—You are under a major deadline, time is money, everyone has been working around the clock, and Betty says, "This is not in my job description." Hearing that phrase is one of the biggest pains you will ever suffer as a manager. Betty is not someone you want on your team. It is possible, though difficult, to turn her attitude around by being clear on both your expectations and the consequences of her actions.

> *The Going the Extra Mile Employee*—Jeannine is your dream employee. She will take that extra shift that no one else wants, make that one more phone call at the end of the day, make the work environment pleasant for others, and develop solutions to make the workflow easier and more efficient. Jeannine takes ownership of her work environment and leaves it better than she found it.

Ask prospective employees for examples of "going the extra mile" in past jobs. The answer will indicate how they'll perform on your team.

Trait #4:

Taking Responsibility—This is probably the least popular choice for most people, yet the most effective. It is so easy to blame others or external circumstances—a teammate, another department, the economy, traffic, weather, gremlins. People avoid taking responsibility because they don't want to look bad: It can be embarrassing. What would people say? What would it cost them? But when they are brave and see beyond the moment, get clear on where they contributed to the issue, it's possible to see other solutions and avoid similar pitfalls in the future.

> *The Pain of Not Taking Responsibility*—Georgia often makes mistakes, big ones. But instead of owning up to them, she is so involved in finding someone or something else to blame, she spends no time trying to correct the mistake or seeing how it can be avoided in the future. This can cost both time and money, as well as destroy harmony in the workplace.

> *The Taking Responsibility Employee*—Rhonda is usually the one you want to groom for leadership. When she goofs up, she comes right to you with the situation. She takes the high road, rather placing blame. She takes responsibility for the problem and starts to work on solutions, showing both confidence and maturity. She learns from her mistake.

Ask the potential hire if they've ever made any major errors at their last job. Find out how they handled it.

Trait #5:

Tolerance—This trait is rarely referred to in business, probably because of how people interpret the word. When I say tolerance, I don't mean be tolerant of behavior that isn't in alignment with company goals.

From a manager's point of view, one of the biggest time suckers is employees bickering, infighting or stirring up conflicts. Think of your team members as if you were in a long-term personal relationship with them. Sure, everyone can be annoying in some way. Rebecca might whistle and not notice it; Carrie brings smelly fish for lunch every day; Katrina talks really loudly on her phone calls. But in a successful work relationship, you have to be committed to team members—annoying traits and all.

You are going to be with your co-workers for at least 40 hours a week, and here's where tolerance comes in.

> *The Pain of Intolerance*—Sylvia is usually fighting, blaming, gossiping, in closed-door meetings, being petty and wasting your time. Not only do you have to deal with her, but you have to meet with the person who she is upset with to soothe those ruffled feathers. She spends a lot of time in your office telling her elaborate story of why the other person has wronged her and how it's not her fault.

> *The Tolerant Employee*—Sandy is a rare gemstone. As the tolerant worker she is the calming force, the voice of reason. Sandy doesn't get her feathers ruffled, and she doesn't ruffle feathers of others. Often she can minimize a conflict and de-escalate it without you even being involved. You hear about it only after the fact.

In my years of management, tolerance was the trait I taught the most. I didn't realize it at the time until I looked back on a culmination of 20 years. And, let me tell you, it *can* be taught. When your team is tolerant of each other, something magical happens. They support each other, they become a work family, they manage their own conflicts, more work gets done and they are laughing. Happy employees yield more productivity, less turnover and a much happier manager, you.

Is this list of valuable long-term traits exclusive? No! There are many more, but these are the traits people don't usually appreciate until they're long gone. As you begin to create your effective, consistent interview system—including questions specific to the candidate's past experiences—you can also incorporate these traits into the list.

Now you are prepared to navigate the interview like a pro. You have techniques to be consistent, you'll be paying attention to clues along the way, you will have a heightened awareness of your own excuses and you will have an idea of valuable long-term traits that you want in your next hire.

In the next chapter you will discover the importance of preparing your new hires for success.

Chapter 2

HIT THE GROUND RUNNING

THE PROPER CARE AND TRAINING OF NEW HIRES: When you are cultivating a team of happy and productive employees, it is important that they start off with a solid foundation. In this chapter you will learn how to create an effective on-boarding plan and training plan.

1. On-boarding Plan
2. Develop a Training Plan

On-boarding Plan

Knowing how much effort, time and money goes into hiring the right employee, my guess is that you want to retain that employee as long as possible. On-boarding is a huge factor in retaining employees and creating a sense of value. That being said, most companies follow the compliance piece of on-boarding, because it's the law, meaning that new hires fill out the proper forms and watch the appropriate safety and compliance videos.

But after that, there is often a gap, and it will be up to you to fill it. To do this, you will need a consistent, thought-out, strategic plan to explain the culture of the company and to involve your new hire in the workplace community—your department. As manager, it is in the best interest of your department for the new hire to feel valued and empowered to be successful right from the start.

I'll paint a picture of a thoughtless, non-strategic on-boarding program. Imagine this scene on your new hire's first day:

> Joanne has made it through all the interviews, the waiting to hear and nail-biting, and it is finally her first day. She's nervous, but excited. She likes the company because it seems like a good fit, and she likes her new boss, a.k.a. you. She is eager to get started, make a great first impression and do a good job. Most of all, Joanne hopes this job will be as good as she was led to believe it would be.
>
> She walks into the office. Where is her desk? Where should she hang up her coat, set her stuff? She's been to the HR department, filled out the forms and is all set to get started. But where is the boss, the one person she knows?
>
> Joanne was thrown into the pool to swim on her own—no life preserver, no lifeguard. It turns out the boss will be in meetings all day. She wanders around looking lost and someone points to an empty desk. She's given basic directions from another coworker, but she is unsure of what is expected of her. So she treads water, wasting both time and money.

OK, this scenario may be a bit exaggerated, but parts of it occur in companies every day. It is critical that you have your new hire's first day planned out. Ultimately, it's your responsibility to see that she feels like a welcome addition to your department.

Remember, your new employee will go home and be asked by loved ones, "How did it go? Did you like it?" What do you want their answer to be?

Here are a few ways to make sure the answers are positive.

Set Up a Welcome Meeting:

I am floored by how many bosses miss this step and then wonder why their employees never understand what they want, talk about them behind their back, slack off, check Facebook throughout the day, and have "doctor's appointments," a.k.a. job interviews, in the middle of the day.

As the direct supervisor, try to set aside at least an hour to meet with your new employee. This isn't just a chit-chat meeting. This is a Welcome Meeting—a time to share your expectations (see Chapter 3) and make sure you set the tone and foundation of your relationship. Your support as their manager is the key to employee retention. The more they feel supported by you, the more you will build loyalty and trust.

Be Prepared:

- Print out your list of job expectations and give it to your newest team members. Go through each point and encourage them to ask questions. It's important that they know they will be heard. And it's important that you are on the same page.
- Ask if they have any expectations, and let them know if they are realistic.
- Find out what motivates them. Do they like a lot of feed-back or do they work better unsupervised? How do they best communicate? Do they prefer scheduled face-time with the boss or will a weekly email report suffice?

Set the Tone:

This meeting is your chance to make your expectations absolutely clear and build a solid foundation for your relationship. It might seem like a big chunk of time. But think about how much time you want to spend training another new hire when this one quits after two months.

Believe me, if you put in the time on the front end, you will save yourself hours of time later reviewing resumes, interviewing, hiring, and training someone all over again. This one little hour on the first day will end up saving you and your company both time and money in the long run.

Always Have a Plan B:

If you cannot make this meeting on their first day, schedule it for some time in the first week. Leave a note on their desk to welcome them, explaining your inability to be there. Then, assign other welcoming tasks to a more senior employee on your team, and be clear about the objective.

Have someone there to:
- Welcome new team members and greet them by name.
- Get them settled and give them a tour.
- Introduce them to relevant staff.
- Give them specific assignments to fill the day, such as study sales scripts, read the company manual, study products, shadow other team members, make practice calls, get logged on to the software, or view instructional videos.

Bonus Ideas That Create a Sense of Value:

1. Have a box of stationery handy in your desk and leave a "Welcome to the Team" card on their desk. If the other team members can sign it, even better!

2. Send an email to the team and other departments welcoming new employees. This way when they are getting the tour, other workers can greet them more personally and the new hires will feel like they already belong.

3. During the team meeting have each co-worker ask the new hires questions about themselves, such as what is their favorite sports team, food, office pet peeve, or type

of music. This creates commonality and collaboration immediately and allows them to feel included even when they don't really know anyone.

But of course, there is more to on-boarding then the first day. You will want to create a plan for new hires to be successful at their jobs, which means job training, sharing cultural norms and welcoming them into the community. Next, we're going to cover the importance of having a training plan.

Develop a Training Plan

There is a big variance in the business world when it comes to training plans and systems. Many large companies have entire departments dedicated to training, but within those companies, the training may be job-related or professional skills-related.

Because most small businesses don't have access to those types of resources, training can often be an afterthought. The fingers-crossed method: "We'll just throw them in there and see how they do," may not be too effective.

That said, here are the basics on how to make the best of your particular training situation. If you work in a smaller company, you can delegate (see Chapter 7) this task or work on it yourself in bite-size pieces. If you are part of a larger company with a training department, you can look for any gaps in what you need and offer solutions on how to improve. Or you can work with me at Employee Management Consulting to determine what the next best step would be for your particular situation.

The absolute ideal solution is to set up your own detailed and systematic process for training a new hire. Don't groan. It will be worth it. You will be able to use this system again and again. Granted, it takes a little work to set it up, but imagine the hours and headaches it will save you later.

Guidelines to Developing your Training Plan:

- Depending on the complexity of the position, plan on up to four weeks for training and implementation. The more there is to learn, the longer it will take.
- Include simple, but important, tasks, such as getting logged on to the system, as well as the heavy duty tasks, such as learning the regulations, studying policies, knowing company products.
- Incorporate meetings with employees in key departments, as necessary.
- Set up a timetable for progress: For example, have their training plan in writing with due dates, and have a set time to meet with them.

I've created a template to get your training plan created for Week One. Your final template may be longer or shorter depending on the scope of the position. Also keep in mind that this can be a fluid document. You are simply getting it started, but you will probably adjust it as you go through it a few times.

Check out the Sample On-Boarding Training Schedule with different training items for Week One. It includes example assignments that are common in most companies.

Divide the sheet into four columns:
1. Task
2. Employee Initials
3. Supervisor Initials
4. Date

This way you have a document that is clearly tracking their progress and involves another person.

Sample On-Boarding Training Schedule

Week One

Task	Employee Initials	Supervisor Initials	Date
Log in to internal software system			
Watch software training modules 1-3			
Meet with key employees in Depts. A, B, C			
Review company website			
Read product manual			
Attend staff meeting			

Note: Download an excel version of this template online at *www.EmployeeManagementConsulting.com/templates*

Make sure that your training schedule is realistic in the amount of time needed to complete each task and that you or another supervisor / mentor is meeting with them each day or week to review the completion, answer questions and provide guidance and support.

Also consider how you would like to invite them into the community and teach them about the company culture.

- **Mentor:** Assign a mentor for the first month and then evaluate to determine the success of their relationship.

- **Social Media:** Are there any social media sites that you use to create employee engagement? If so, invite them to join.
- **Outside Activities:** Are there any outside of work activities, such as community service projects, 10K walks or sports activities that team members participate in? Invite them to join.
- **Other Departments:** Have you included interaction or cross-training with other departments? This key component creates a sense of value for both the new employee and the others involved in the training.

You are now well-equipped to start developing successful On-Boarding and Training Plans that will cultivate happy and productive employees. Next you will discover the power of creating clear expectations for your employees.

Chapter 3

THEY CAN'T READ YOUR MIND

BE CLEAR ABOUT YOUR EXPECTATIONS: As a successful manager, it is critical that you learn how to recognize, list and communicate your expectations effectively and authentically. Many managers make the big mistake of having unclear expectations and communicating them when the damage has been done and there is no turning back. Rise to the top 10% of successful managers who lead with authenticity and a high level of effective communication. In this chapter we are going to cover the Top 3 Mistakes to avoid when it comes to your expectations.

1. Unclear or Unknown Expectations
2. Keeping your Expectations a Secret
3. Communicating Your Expectations Ineffectively

Mistake #1:
Unclear or Unknown Expectations

One of the biggest mistakes managers make is having unclear or unknown expectations for their staff.

Why is this a problem? And if it's such a big problem, why isn't every manager clear on his or her expectations? The answer is, it's a problem because people need to be guided or they will make up their own plan. Imagine that your employees don't know when to come in to work, what to do when they get there or what the company policies are. They would be dazed and confused, non-productive and ineffective, right? And who could blame them?

Would you expect them to hit the ground running and start making these decisions on their own? Probably not, because most people will choose the easiest path for them. They will come in when they feel like it, get started working when they feel like it, call the number of clients they feel like calling, and ignore the tasks that they don't feel like doing. And to make matters worse, each employee will have a different plan.

Cleaning up that mess will end up costing you a lot of time and effort. You will also end up looking for new workers, because this group won't hit their numbers. If employees are making it up as they go along, what are the chances that you will have several different perceptions of what the "right way" is? Very high!

Instead, imagine you are in the top 10% percent of high-quality managers. You are clear on what type of expectations you have of your staff, and you have an effective way to communicate your expectations.

As a result, you lower the level of confusion and ambiguity on your team. You have workers who are clear about their purpose and can hit the ground running. You also have a strong foundation to stand on when your expectations are not met. In effect, you have paved the road for direct communication, mutual purpose and agreement up front. This will save you hours of hassle in the future.

Plus, as you hire new employees, you can communicate these expectations from the beginning. You will also come up with a plan for "teaching old dogs new tricks."

Solution: *Develop a clear set of expectations for your staff*

This may sound like an obvious or easy assignment. And for those of you who already have clarity on your expectations, this will be a piece of cake. But if you haven't got a list going, then you are in luck. I have developed a list of **10 Questions** to ask yourself to determine your expectations of employees. The answers to these questions are not the expectations you are necessarily going to share with your staff, but some of them may be.

For example, imagine you live with another person, and you don't see eye-to-eye on doing the dishes. What is your expectation in terms of doing the dishes? Do you want the other person to do the dishes if you do the cooking or vice-versa? Do you enjoy or dislike doing the dishes? Do you have a particular way you like the dishes washed or stacked in the dishwasher? Are you OK if dirty dishes sit in the sink or on the counter for a couple of days? Hours? Minutes?

You probably have answers to all of these questions. But if you ask 10 people, they will all have different expectations about something as simple and harmless as doing the dishes. And do people argue or lose sleep over something as simple as doing the dishes? Yes! We don't walk around with a book of expectations written out—sometimes we don't even know what they are until those expectations are not met.

That's why this process is so important. Think about what makes you proud of your employees, your pet peeves and what upsets you. Those will help uncover hidden expectations. This is not an exhaustive list, but it will help you build a great foundation.

10 Questions to Determine Your Expectations

1. What time do you want them at the desk and ready to go?
2. What should they do if they are going to be late due to traffic, family emergencies, health issues or the like?
3. What are your thoughts about punctuality?
4. Do you walk the walk? Are you a role model of your expectations? In what ways?
5. What is the culture of the office or department?
6. What is the most important priority?
7. Do you have a win-win philosophy? Describe it.
8. Who should they go to if they have questions?
9. When you think of your core values or work ethic, what comes to mind?
10. What are their daily responsibilities?

I understand this is a lot to consider, but do you see how important it is for you to bring these expectations to light? If you have not considered what is important to you, how in the world will your employees know what you expect?

Here are two expectation examples:

Expectation 1:

I have a "WIN x 4" philosophy: Whenever possible, my goal is to have a WIN-WIN-WIN-WIN for you, me, the client, and the company. This does not always happen, but if my team thinks in this manner, we have a higher chance of making it happen.

Expectation 2:

My expectation is that you are on time and ready to work. Being on time does not mean pulling into the parking lot at 8 a.m. and then getting your coffee and chatting with your co-workers. It means you are at your desk ready to get your workday started at 8 a.m.

To-Do: Take a moment and write out some of your own expectations in the "NOTES" section at the back of your book.

Mistake #2:
Keeping Your Expectations a Secret

You are already one step ahead because you have some questions to ask yourself and are on your way to knowing what your expectations are. That is the step most people miss altogether. But after you have compiled your list and gotten clarity, there is another crucial step. You need to communicate those expectations to your staff.

Why would some people decide not to communicate this important information to their staff? Well, for lots of reasons, unfortunately.

They may:
- Not know.
- Not care.
- Think it is letting go of control.
- Be insecure.
- Not feel comfortable telling people what to do.
- Whether you are a manager or an employee, you are ultimately human. And you will do what feels most comfortable and put off or ignore the rest when left to your own devices.

But you are taking a step beyond that. You want to be a great leader for your staff. Possibly you want to grow professionally and be promoted or perhaps have your own business one day. You care about the people you manage and want to create a happy and productive work environment. That's why you are willing to invest in your growth and go through steps to up your game.

Solution: *Be Clear About What and Why You Are Communicating*

Once you have completed your list of expectations, prepare it in a format that you can share with your employees. But before you send it off in a mass email—don't do that—take a step back and p-a-u-s-e. Yes, it is critical that you are clear on your expectations and that you share them. But *what* and *why* you share are also critical. You don't want to send the wrong message and create a big mess to clean up.

WHAT you share:

There are some basics in terms of "what" you share, and I'm going to give you guidance in this area. Ultimately, though, this will be a document unique to you. Who you are as a manager, what is important to you, the culture of your department and company, your staff, your job and your responsibilities will encompass this document.

10 Areas to Cover to Develop Your Expectations

1. *Overall job description*—In your words, what do you expect the employee to accomplish each day, week, month, quarter, year?
2. *Attitude*—What are your thoughts or opinions about negativity in the workplace?
3. *Work Ethic*—What do you expect out of employees in terms of work ethic?
4. *Punctuality*—It is critical that you are very clear about what you mean by being on time.
5. *Open Door Policy*—How do they know when to come to you? What type of communication is appropriate when they need your advice?
6. *Conflict Management*—What is the norm? How do you expect them to manage conflicts? With other employees? With you? HR? Customers?
7. *Personal Issues*—What is OK and not OK to share? What type of culture is the norm? Is it a family environment where everyone knows everyone's business, or is it more formal—come in, do your job and leave?
8. *Evaluations*—How often do you review staff? What criteria will they be reviewed by? What is the typical pay increase?
9. *Your Pet Peeves*—The way to get on my bad side is ...
10. *What You Admire In Your Staff*—What characteristics do you think are top notch?

Because I don't know what your expectations are, I cannot tell you exactly what to say or not say. If we end up working together through Employee Management Consulting, then we would go through them together. If you are flying solo, make sure to share your list with a couple of people you trust and respect before you share it with your employees.

Why? You may think your expectations are totally acceptable and make 100% sense. But if you are sharing them with your employees, you don't know how they will be interpreted. The last thing you want to do is alienate and / or offend your employees. This communication is important and can make or break you.

WHY you are sharing:

Ask yourself this question, "Why is it important for me to share my expectations with my employees?" Your answers may be something like ...

> *"So they know when they are doing a good job, and to lessen misunderstandings."*

> *"To have effective evaluation meetings."*

> *"So everyone knows what they are supposed to do and there are minimal surprises."*

> *"To create a supportive team environment."*

I doubt that your reason for sharing is to make yourself feel important, throw your weight around, and create a feeling of fear or micromanagement.

Whatever your WHY is, get clear on it. What problem are you solving? What future problems are you preventing? Where are you setting people up for success? How can you lay a foundation that will help you save hours of time rehiring and writing up people for poor performance?

I understand that setting up all of these steps may not be as easy as it sounds. You may have special circumstances that cloud which direction you can go and what changes you can implement.

But my purpose is to make your management life one that works for you: A life where you feel accomplished, successful and proud of what you do. A life with balance and ease, in which you lead others to great success efficiently and with integrity. I know that each scenario, heck, each employee, is unique. When I work one-on-one with my clients, we dig deep into these scenarios and come up with creative ways to succeed.

Mistake #3:
Communicating Your Expectations
Ineffectively

Ineffective communication can actually be more damaging than not communicating at all. Why? Because when people experience anything new there is often resistance. When you do something different as a manager—communicate something you've never communicated before—count on some backlash. If the goal is happy and productive employees, then you will want to be mindful of how you go about it, what you say and in what format you wish to communicate to get the best outcome. What your best outcome is, will be up to you.

Here are two expectation styles:

Expectation Style 1:

For example, if you are experiencing low productivity due to an ingrained culture of tardiness, you will want to determine how to deliver your message to get immediate change. You might need to wake people up, lay down the law and share the clear consequences of tardiness moving forward.

Expectation Style 2:

Alternatively, perhaps you have a healthy functioning team. They have been working really hard and are on the verge of burning out due to a big project and massive overtime. Your approach may come from a place of gratitude and inspiration, and asking them what they need to keep pushing forward.

Do you see by these two contrasting examples, that how you communicate may vary?

When you have a final draft that you feel is professional and will bring about the results you desire, you can decide how you want to communicate your expectations. You may elect to share them in a one-on-one session with each employee, so you can create a safe space for dialogue. How you take this next step will depend on the size of your staff, your time and the culture of your company.

I do not recommend sending your expectation list in an email, and definitely not a mass email. Email doesn't provide the nonverbal and verbal cues that a face-to-face conversation does. The recipient will not be able to hear your tonality, pitch, volume or kindness. You can present them in written form, but only if you are there to explain and walk through each item. The context of this meeting should be safe and supportive rather than punitive.

Therefore, I suggest you increase your mindfulness and awareness of what is most important for your staff to know and why it is important. What do you think will work best? What has worked for you in the past? Do you have certain people on the team who are highly influential? It may be easier to get them on board first, and let them steer the others toward compliance.

Do you have someone who is highly sensitive to change? You may have to plan for extra time with that person. Do you have a situation where you think the whole team can hear the message together? You can set up a team session for an overview, and then follow with individual meetings if necessary. Your situation will be different depending on the number of people you are managing.

Solution: *Create a Fool-Proof Expectation Delivery System*

At this point you may have had a chance to complete your list of expectations, answer the questions and determine what expectations you need to communicate to your staff. Some people prefer to read the entire chapter and then go back and complete the steps after they've read the whole thing. Either way is fine.

When you start creating your Fool-Proof Expectation Delivery System, you will want to have answered the questions about your expectations and decided what you want to share with your staff.

You will compile information about yourself and your team, and then put a realistic plan in place. The questions below are designed to help you frame your strategy and keep you focused.

10 Questions for Creating Your Fool-Proof Expectation Delivery System:

1. How many people do you currently manage?
2. What has been your strategy been, so far, in communicating your expectations?
3. What worked? What didn't work?
4. Who would be a good resource to provide feedback about your expectations, other than your staff? Develop a plan to get the advice of someone you know, like and trust. If you don't have anyone who meets those characteristics, you can work with me.
5. Do you have regularly scheduled staff or employee meetings? If so, when? How? For what purpose? Is it appropriate to communicate your expectations in one of these meetings?
6. What medium will you use to communicate? Face-to-face, phone, conference, meeting or other?
7. Who do you need to hear your message?
8. What materials do you need to have developed? PowerPoint, a sheet of paper, or simply your notes?
9. How will you include the expectation list in your on-boarding process for new hires?

10. What is a reasonable deadline for your communication to
    be completed?
    a. If it's a group meeting, when is your meeting date
       and time?
    b. If you are meeting with individuals, what blocks
       of time do you need in order to meet with each
       of them?

To-Do: This session is heavy on the homework because you are
laying a foundation that will pay off for the rest of your career.
Here's a recap of your homework:

1. Be clear about your expectations. Use the list of
   prompting questions and come up with your own,
   as needed.
2. Write up your list of expectations to share with your staff.
3. Get feedback prior to communicating your expectations,
   and allow time for revisions.
4. Create a Fool-Proof Expectation Delivery System that
   works for your staff.
5. Communicate your expectations.

As you can probably tell by now, knowing and communicating your
expectations appropriately are absolutely critical to your success as
a manager. The clearer you are, the easier it will be to coach your
team and keep them on the right track. In the next chapter you
will learn to empower others by creating a sense of value.

Chapter 4

SHOW THE LOVE

CREATE A SENSE OF VALUE: Would you like your staff to feel valued so they are productive, responsible, hardworking and loyal? All with a positive attitude? The goal of this chapter is to end sleepless nights of stress, burning the candles at both ends and negativity in the workplace. It starts by empowering others by creating a sense of value in them. The two areas that you will learn in this chapter are how to:

1. Create a Sense of Value Immediately
2. Create a Sense of Value for the Long Term

Create a Sense of Value Immediately

Did you know that approximately 60% of workers are dissatisfied? You might even be one of them. Your employees might be some of them, too. Did you also know that the cost of replacing employees is estimated at 200% of their salary? You don't need to be a mathematician to figure out that replacing your employees can cost you a tremendous amount of time and money—two of your most valuable resources.

How would creating a sense of value in your employees make your life easier?

The answer is simple: If you want happy, productive employees who stay, then their sense of value is critical for your team's success.

What creates a sense of value for employees?

The answers may be different from what you might immediately assume is of the highest importance: big paychecks.

In fact, employees experience a greater sense of value when they:
- Feel appreciated and included.
- Believe that you care about them personally, not just professionally.

Clearly, it is important to find out what your employees value—both as a team and individually. How can you tell if they feel valued? Following is a list of solutions and tips on how to create a sense of value. This is not an exhaustive list, by any means. And because each staff and individual worker is different, you may want put your own spin on it.

This first method is a biggie. It's so easy, so simple that you have probably done it many times and completely forgotten about it just as many times. That's why I'm going over it now.

This method is free, easy and can be done anywhere. I'm revealing the **Biggest Secret in Business** to create a sense of value and keep your employees loyal to you and the company, and in love with their job. Are you ready?

The Biggest Secret in Business is...

Say, Thank You!

If they do something outside of their job description, go the extra mile, hit a big goal, help you in some way, or are just in need of a pick-me-up, a simple thank you goes a long way. A verbal, sincere, authentic and specific thank you will pay off for a long time. By saying thank you, you are showing appreciation, showing that you see them and that they matter. How many times have you done something great and no one noticed or acknowledge you? It stinks, doesn't it? Most people feel the same way.

9 Tips to Create a Sense of Value

1. If they helped another employee, encourage that employee to give a public thank you at the next staff meeting.
2. Acknowledge them at the next team meeting.
3. Email them a video of their favorite song.
4. Find a way to make a project fun.
5. Create a friendly competition.
6. Make a game out of a tedious project.
7. Set up a reward system.
8. Ask them for their input on a new initiative.
9. Give them credit for a good idea they contributed.

Now take a few minutes to create your own list of ways to create a sense of value in your employees. Think about the individuals you manage. What do you think they would need to feel valued? If you don't know, ask them and then begin to formulate your ideas.

At this point you have begun to understand why creating a sense of value is so critical—because it is saving you massive amounts of time and money replacing employees. And now you have lots of techniques to begin creating a sense of value in your employees.

Create a Sense of Value for the Long Term

In order to create a sense of value in others for the long term, you will construct your long-term vision.

What is your long-term vision?

Depending on your role—owner or manager—the length of time will be different. Select a date that you know where you want your department, division, company to be. For example, within a year's time, our company / department / goal will be X. If you are the owner of the company, your long-term vision may be 5 or 10 years down the road. Select a time frame that works for you and that you can share with your staff.

Take a moment now and write out your long-term vision. Be as detailed as you can. You will want to include details about:

- Profit
- Growth
- Projects completed
- Marketing strategies
- New products / services
- Size of the company / departments
- Your role
- Customer / client experience
- Supporting the company mission
- Other goals

Next, you will need to create a plan to share your long-term vision. Remember, you are creating a sense of value so that your employees feel included, on-board, excited, supportive and supported. Knowing yourself, the company culture and your staff, what do you think would be the best way to share the long-term vision?

Prepare to Share Your Long-Term Vision

1. Who would benefit from knowing my long-term vision?
2. What part(s) of the vision would be effective to share?
3. Why is it important for me to share the long-term vision?
4. How will this information affect the staff, and how can this communication create a sense of value for my staff?

Next, imagine that next week you were prepared to make this communication. What would it look like? Are you leading a meeting with the entire department? Giving a PowerPoint presentation? How did the meeting get set up? Where will it be held?

Employees who feel that they are part of the process will have a sense of ownership and a higher degree of engagement. Therefore, they are more likely to be committed to the goal, i.e., more dedicated and responsible. And when your employees feel valued, they are more likely to be more productive, happy and loyal. This makes your job more rewarding, too. It's a win-win situation.

In order to maintain the fruits of your labor in both creating and sharing your long-term vision, remember two key follow-up support strategies:

2 Key Follow-Up Support Strategies

1. *Involve your staff in decisions when possible:*
   As you review your long-term vision, where might you need support? Are you planning on accomplishing it alone? Probably not. You will need the resources and talent of your staff. Assuming you have some talent on your staff, involve them. Form committees, delegate, ask questions, ask for feedback, put someone in charge of something, and ask who wants to be involved. This is a golden opportunity to increase both their level of engagement and their sense of value.

2. *Keep the vision top of mind:*
   Have you ever been a part of a company that had a big fancy announcement about a new initiative or promise only never to hear of it again? I have. Lots of promises and dreams and fanfare, followed by a void. This is not very motivating, effective or strategic. So if you are going to put this effort in, which is valuable and has the potential to be very effective, you'll need to keep the vision alive and top of mind.

What does that look like for you? Here are some questions to guide you in creating a consistent message.

- What form of communication do you want to use to keep the vision alive? Some choices are: email, posters / signage, marketing, messaging, social media, staff meetings, committees.
- Who can you ask to help you?
- What resources do you have that will make this effective?
- Looking out on the next 12 months, where / how will you keep this vision alive?
- What resources do you need that you don't have? How will you get them??

By now, you have an understanding of why it is so important for your employees to have a sense of value. You also have a short-term, more immediate list of ideas to implement as well as a strategy to develop and share your long-term vision. Both your short-term and long-term plans will increase the sense of value in your employees. In the next chapter you will learn strategies on how to coach your team.

Chapter 5

FINGER ON THE PULSE

COACHING YOUR TEAM: To be a successful manager, it's absolutely critical to hang on to your quality employees. Hiring and training can be your No. 1 time sucker and stressor. This chapter will cover three simple strategies to increase the likelihood of employees staying and result in creating a safe place for your staff to grow and succeed.

1. Show Them You Care
2. Know When to Build Them Up
3. Know When to Push for More

Strategy #1:
Show Them You Care

There's a saying, "They don't care how much you know until they know how much you care." It's true. If your staff doesn't think you care about them, guess what, they will be much less inclined to go the extra mile for you.

Example:
One of the teams I managed required phone coverage for 12 hours a day, including Saturdays. That meant that the staff requirements had to be flexible over the regular 8 to 5 shift. And Saturdays had

to be covered, too. There were also frequent special events when attendance was required and vacation was not permitted.

Over time, each member of my staff had a significant life event that took precedence over work—wedding, baby, funeral, flu, car problems. They were working so many hours that the odds of life interfering were pretty high. So I listened, and when I could accommodate them, I would. They didn't always get what they asked for, but because I cared about them as people, not just as employees, they gave me 150%. I also was there by their side as they worked on those required days.

5 Easy Ways to Show You Care

1. Take time to ask about their lives outside of work.
2. Check in with them during your one-on-one meetings.
3. If you notice someone seems a little off, you can say, "Is everything OK?"
4. Establish an open-door policy, and mean it.
5. Create a safe environment for ideas to be shared.

If they feel like they can trust you, they will give back to you, they will care more about their job, and they will be happier and more productive. They will share their ideas with you, and your department / team / company will benefit.

It's important to allow your employees to feel safe to share their ideas, because you don't have every great idea ever invented. Even if you already have goals, it's important to involve your staff in the goal-setting process when possible. This creates an opportunity for new ideas to be expressed and heard. It also creates an opportunity for questions or obstacles to be discussed. Have a team meeting, or quick huddle, on a regular basis to encourage the flow of ideas and questions.

Strategy #2:
Know When to Build Them Up

The more you have gotten to know your staff, the more in tune you will be when they need your support. Sometimes people just had a bad day, got hung-up on for the 10th time in a row, or got yelled at by a client. Here's where being in tune with your top performers can pay off tremendously!

- Abby may just need a quick, "How are you doing, really?" and 30 seconds to get something off her chest.
- Lauren may be more sensitive. She might need a one-on-one meeting in your office, giving her time to get whatever it is out of her system, re-energize, and get back out on the floor.
- Nanette might need a good joke, a funny YouTube video or hearing her favorite song.

When the whole team's energy is circling the drain, you would be surprised how much productivity a couple of pizzas or a coffee run will bring. If the team inspires each other, get them in a quick huddle and have them share success stories.

Your manager's intuition is critical for this step. Knowing how to motivate not only each person, but the team as a whole is price-less. Feelings fuel our actions, so if the feelings are low, the actions are going to be less effective. By you building them up, you will show them they are valued, and they will be more likely to pro-duce the results you seek.

Browbeating them when they are already down is not only inef-fective, it's likely to produce negative results. They will be resentful, stressed and probably polishing up their resumes as soon as you turn your back. That being said, sometimes you will simply have to get them to the next level and motivate them to dig deeper right away.

Strategy #3:
Know When to Push for More

Just like any great coach, you are there to push your team beyond what they believe they are capable of doing.

You'll know it's time to push if you notice a certain lull or lackadaisical mood in your department. There's no buzz. Energy is blah. People are leaning over cubicles and talking about the latest reality TV show. That is the perfect time to Walk The Floor (see Chapter 6). Sometimes that's all it takes to redirect the focus back to the tasks at hand.

But other times, you may need them to pull something out of their hat because time is running out. There's a lot of pressure from higher up, and everyone is feeling stressed. Here's where the foundation you have laid will pay off instantly. This is when you, as their leader, can get honest and tough. Call them together and give them your pitch.

> *Sample script:*
>
> "OK, team, we have a big goal in front of us. I know we are all under a lot of pressure right now, but I also know that each and every one of you can make this happen. We need to go the extra mile today—or for the next hour, week, month. That means we have to support each other in staying on task. If someone starts chatting to you about anything besides a work-related issue, gently remind them of our goal. Can we all agree to keep each other accountable?"

And then, you will want to follow up. Have them say to the rest of the team what they are committed to contributing. If you have been doing this regularly they won't be shy or shell-shocked. Telling their contribution to their co-workers results in a psychological pressure that will work wonders for them. For those who aren't contributing equally, it just got aired. For those who regularly carry their weight, they will push for more. The less productive ones will have a chance to change their fate. In the end, everyone benefits.

When you involve your staff in the goal, vision, or big picture—and let them know that you are counting on each and every one of them—they will feel valued and noticed. Lead them to victory and involve them in the process so they can feel the celebration of success as a team. Decide as a group on what type of celebration you would like to have when the goal is achieved. Finally, give the team some parameters in terms of budget and appropriate celebration activities.

Each time you do this, the staff members will bond and create memories that solidify the experience for the next time.

- They will start to build each other up.
- They will come to you with ideas without you having to ask.
- They will pitch in without being told. Your life will become easier as your staff becomes more productive.
- Your stress will lessen, and you will have more time for the big picture.

Now you are prepared with strategies you can utilize, depending on what your team needs. At times, you will show them you care, know when to build them up and know when to push for more. In the next chapter you will learn two communication strategies you can use to be a successful manager.

Chapter 6
SAY WHAT?

EFFECTIVE COMMUNICATION: In this chapter you will learn two simple and effective communication techniques you can implement immediately. Poor communication leaves you vulnerable to significant risk—ideas are not expressed and you can lose quality people—leading to more stress, wasted time and lower productivity and profitability. The two secrets in this chapter helped me tremendously in having effective communication with my staff, and they will help you, too! Here they are:

1. Perception Checking
2. Walk The Floor

Communication Secret #1:
Perception Checking

If you have never heard of Perception Checking, then today is your lucky day. This is a super simple skill to understand and teach to your staff. It may sound a little hokey at first, but in truth it's very powerful. And you can make it a fun way to increase the effectiveness of the communication in the workplace.

You have your own unique perceptions of reality. And I'm guessing that you typically think your perception is the correct one. If you have siblings, I'm sure there has been one point in your life when you argued about the facts of a memory. You are certain that it happened one way, and your sibling is equally certain it happened a different way. If only there were a time machine. But there isn't, so you'll have to settle for increasing your perception awareness.

I learned about Perception Checking upon taking my first interpersonal communication class. While earning a Master's degree in Speech Communication, I then had the chance to teach this concept to undergraduate students. It was my favorite skill to teach because of its simplicity and effectiveness. You can use it in all kinds of situations with no prep or checking your notes.

The goal of Perception Checking is to minimize misunderstanding, conflict and confusion. The idea is to check your interpretation of someone else's message, rather than assume that your interpretation is correct. For example, you may sense that the person you are speaking to is upset, but you're not sure if that is true. You would check in with them to see if your perception is accurate or if something else is going on. Using this skill empowers you to significantly reduce misunderstandings and conflicts that occur when you assume a meaning that differs from the intended meaning.

Here are the three simple steps to Perception Checking, followed with a couple of examples to help you get the idea of how it plays out in real-life scenarios.

3 Steps to Perception Checking

1. **Description of the behavior:** Describe what you noticed.
2. **Interpretation:** Share two possible interpretations of the behavior or communication you noticed.
3. **Ask for Clarification:** Did you understand correctly or was another message intended?

It is important to note a couple of things before you try out Perception Checking on your co-workers. You need to be highly aware of your nonverbal communication, such as tone of voice, how loudly you are speaking, and how high-pitched your voice might be getting.

If you perform any of the three steps with an attitude or an irritable tone in your voice you might be headed for trouble. When emotions are high, intelligence plummets. Make sure you are curious and open to your interpretation being inaccurate. It's essential that you are open to the idea that the other person might have a completely different meaning.

Here are some typical examples that could occur in the workplace.

Scenario 1—*Your employee had told you a sale would close by Tuesday. It's Wednesday, and she hasn't let you know if it went through or not.*

1. **Description:** Hi, Susie. I didn't hear from you about the close of the sale.
2. **Interpretation:** I thought it was going to close on Tuesday and then got concerned when I didn't get an update from you. I was wondering if you had meant to communicate to me, but forgot.
3. **Clarification:** What's the current status?

Try to imagine the different possibilities here. Perhaps ...

- Susie closed the sale on Tuesday and has been working to complete all the required paperwork, but forgot to update you.
- She didn't close the sale and was dreading giving you the bad news.
- There is a message from the client that they want to close the sale, but Susie hasn't been able to reach them.
- The client never showed up or called back.

When you allow your imagination to open up to the possibilities, you start to realize that you actually have no idea what is accurate. When you get attached to your interpretations and are unwilling to entertain other perceptions, you become closed off to people, ideas, creativity and productivity. You can create resentment, conflict, chaos and waste time and energy.

Scenario 2 — *You checked to see if your employee was on track with her project, because you suspect she hasn't started and is behind schedule.*

1. **Description:** Hi, Carol. You said you would complete the project, but I heard that it hasn't been started. I haven't heard from you about it.
2. **Interpretation:** I thought you might need help or that maybe you forgot about it.
3. **Clarification:** Is it possible I'm missing something?

Now, as you hear this example, you can tell how important it is to have your nonverbal communication in check. Read differently, this example could elicit major attitude. And if this is in an email, there are no verbal cues at all.

If you truly believed the project was behind schedule and Carol had dropped the ball, you would probably have a negative reaction. This is when Perception Checking can be the most effective.

Your thoughts generate feelings, and your feelings then generate more thoughts at a very rapid pace. I bet that if you truly thought that Carol didn't follow through with the project your thoughts might be something like, "I can't believe she hasn't started! I trusted her! Now, we are going to miss our deadline!" Which means your feelings might be anger, disgust, irritation, and betrayal.

So how in the heck do you use this simple Perception Checking technique when you are feeling this way?

This is when it pays to work on yourself long before approaching Carol. Acknowledge the assumed perceptions you have and the feelings you have based on those assumptions. Take responsibility for your feelings. And then ask, "What else might be possible?" I am sure I'm not the only one who has ever been wrong about someone's intentions. Remember, there are loads of possibilities. You can play the possibilities game in your mind.

It goes like this. Maybe....

- Carol started the project and it is locked in her safe at home so no one can steal it.
- She was up all night working on it and hasn't told anyone yet.
- She's afraid of admitting she needs help.
- Her mom is gravely ill, and she's barely holding it together.
- She won the lottery and is going to give her notice the day the check arrives.

You won't know what is going on until you actually check in with Carol.

Now, don't get me wrong. It's not like everyone gets a free pass and all the excuses in the world are OK. No, no, no. But you want to have clarity before getting caught up in your perceptions and the fantasy that your perceptions are reality. Once you get clarity with the other person, you can renegotiate, resolve or move forward as needed.

Communication Secret #2
Walk The Floor

I am going to share with you one of the best employee retention communication secrets I have used as a manager. I call it WTF.

WTF, in this context, means "Walk The Floor." As a manager, you are probably very busy attending multiple meetings and trying to achieve your team goals, motivate your staff and reassure your clients. There is a quick and easy way to find out what's really going on with your staff and how you can motivate them to stay positive and focused on their goals. Just, Walk The Floor.

You might be thinking, that's it? That's all I'm supposed to do is just walk around? How is that going to help me gain team commitment and increase productivity? Sounds like a waste of time. Well, you won't just walk around aimlessly. You'll have a strategy. I'm going to give you a few to try until you develop what works best for you.

Walk The Floor is meant to be fun by getting you out of your tunnel vision of focusing only on your own goals. If you are depending on your staff and other departments to help accomplish your goals, then there is significant value in creating positive relationships with others. If your only focus is "me, me, me" then you will have a challenging time when you need the support of co-workers. You'll need to practice giving, so that you can receive and thereby create reciprocal relationships. Here are some strategies to get you started.

Walk The Floor Strategies

1. **Forecast:** Find out what they are up to that day: Any big accounts getting ready to close?
2. **Problem Solve:** Are they facing any challenges?
3. **Preventative Maintenance:** Any gossip brewing or in-fighting that you need to be aware of so you can nip it before it implodes?
4. **Build Trust:** They will feel like you care.
5. **Create Accountability / Celebration of Wins:** How did that client meeting go? Did you get the sale? High five!
6. **Collaborate:** Do they need any support from you?
7. **Mentor:** Share your experience in the challenge they are facing.
8. **Gentle Reminder:** Upcoming meetings or company goals.
9. **Build Rapport:** Invite them to share what they like to do outside of work. What do you have in common?

Walk The Floor Scenarios

1. Sit down at their cube and chat for a couple of minutes.
2. Ask questions. Keep it light, but if they need private time with you, offer it when possible.
3. Give acknowledgement or thanks, if appropriate.
4. Wander into the break room or wherever your employees tend to gather.
5. Take different routes to your office each day. This allows you to see a variety of people over the course of a week.
6. Purposely go through a different department to connect with people you don't normally see. This is a great time to say, "Hi," and check in with them. If you stay connected, then when you need their support it won't be like you're starting from scratch.

Your Customized Walk the Floor Game Plan

- What ways can you Walk The Floor?
- Where would you go?
- Who would you talk to?
- When would be the best time for you to Walk The Floor?
- How often?

Now you have two powerful Successful Manager Communication Secrets to pull out of your back pocket and implement immediately. Start practicing your Perception Checking, teach it to your staff and create some fun role-playing exercises at the next meeting. Then create your WTF strategy to see what information you discover and how you can increase your opportunities to problem-solve. In the next chapter you will learn how to use the power of delegation.

Chapter 7

GET PEOPLE TO DO STUFF

DELEGATION IS YOUR BEST FRIEND: Delegation is much more than telling people what to do. When done successfully, delegation is an act of allowing another to feel responsible and empowered. When faced with the choice to delegate or not, managers often face obstacles, such as lack of control, lack of trust in the other person and lack of time to train someone how to do the task properly. This chapter shows you how to overcome these challenges so you can become a highly successful leader and cover the following:

1. Obstacles to delegation.
2. Overcoming delegation obstacles.
3. Time-saving strategies.
4. Develop your delegation plan.
5. Implement your delegation plan.

Obstacles to Delegation

This step in your delegation plan is crucial. If there were no obstacles, then everyone would be delegating all the time. Most people think it's a great idea, but there are definitely obstacles unique to you and your particular situation.

4 Big Obstacles to Delegation:
1. Trust
2. Control
3. Time
4. Lack of Clarity or Training

Which of these obstacles resonate for you? Where do you get stuck and why? What would help you through those obstacles: A new perspective? An honest conversation? Time designated to train someone? The more clarity and honesty you have about what is true for you, the quicker you can overcome these obstacles.

Big Obstacle #1: TRUST

How many times have you caught yourself saying or thinking that you are the only one who can do the task? You are the best one for the job. Your way is the best way. Whenever you let someone else take over they screw it up.

This type of thinking indicates a lack of trust, and trust is a huge factor in delegation. Depending on the task, the trust factor may take a long time to develop. You are wise to be mindful when you trust others, especially when the risk is high. But you also want to increase your awareness of why you hold back in delegating.

Get Honest With Yourself:
- Are you hoarding tasks and responsibilities so you can get all the credit?
- Are you working 12-hour days, skipping meals and letting your health be affected because you don't trust anyone else to get the job done?
- Are you stockpiling vacation days, because you dare not leave your work to others?

This is where it's essential to look within and get honest with your personal issues with trust. When have you been let down in the past? On the other hand, when have you been able to trust and it went well?

The first step in overcoming this obstacle is getting clear on your own issues and seeing if they apply to the current situation. If so, it might be necessary to put some extra safety-net steps in place. You may need to follow up, oversee, and have the staff member report back regularly, or check in on a regular basis to determine if the delegation is a success.

Big Obstacle #2: CONTROL

Managers are typically people who like to be in control. They also are natural leaders—the ones who people look to when no one knows what to do. They are not afraid of taking control. There are benefits to this quality. But when it comes to delegation, many managers experience a high level of resistance to letting go of control.

Real Fears if You Give Up Control:
- Others will make a costly mistake.
- Others might do a better job.
- You will lose touch with your daily operations.
- You could relinquish some of your authority.

In the matter of control it's essential to understand when it is OK or not OK to let go of some of the control. Start by evaluating your staff, selecting the best members to empower or promote. Ease into it by giving them a little bit of control at first, allowing for some evidence of success. This method also gives you a measure of how the delegation process truly affects you.

Big Obstacle #3: TIME

How many times have you heard yourself say that you would delegate if only you had enough time to train someone else? Well, this is totally in your control. Remember, you have the same amount of time as everyone else on the planet. If the President of the United States has time to delegate, then so do you. The good news is, the time you put into this now will actually solve your problem of "not having enough time."

As a manager, the solution to freeing up your time is to spend time you do have on creating systems that make your job easier. It sounds contradictory, but it is true. If you are running too thin on time, it means you need to bring in support to ease the load.

Big Obstacle #4: LACK of CLARITY or TRAINING

This is a tricky obstacle. Sometimes because of lack of trust, resistance to letting go of control and over-maxed time constraints, managers are not always clear when to delegate. Others times they don't provide enough training to set someone up for success.

So as you get honest with yourself about the other three obstacles, take this one into consideration and set yourself up to be a successful delegator.

- What kind of clarity do you need to give?
- What kind of training needs to be in place?
- What part of the training, if any, can be delegated?

If you don't set up the delegated individual for success, then you will end up starting all over again. It's like building a house on a poor foundation. You might have gotten the house built quicker, but it falls apart. Do yourself a favor and nail this one: Give clear directions and expectations with the intention of setting your employee up for success.

Overcoming Delegation Obstacles

Take a moment to consider which obstacles might be in the way of your willingness to delegate. Remember, your ability to work through these obstacles will provide you an easier and more effective work-life balance in the future.

Take special note of the feelings that come up when you think about these obstacles. The strongest feeling fuels the action. So if you are dreading delegation or are coming from a place of fear or mistrust, those feelings will keep you in the same place of doing too much, being stressed and not having time for yourself. This may also lead to team unrest and threaten employee retention.

A good way to experience different feelings is to change your attitude about delegating. Here are some examples of different thoughts to consider as you start to develop your own:

5 New Thoughts about Delegation

1. When I delegate, I will be empowering my staff to succeed.
2. New leaders will emerge as I delegate, and I will have a clearer picture of who I can depend on.
3. I will be able to practice asking for help and allowing others to feel responsible.
4. I won't be just feeding people fish; I will be teaching them how to fish!
5. With all of my extra time after delegating I will be able to focus on the big picture, take care of myself, do some strategic planning, and get home early.

Time-Saving Strategies

As a manager, I know that you are busy, busy, busy. Here are eight strategies you can start using today to save time.

8 Time-Saving Strategies

- Automation
- Train Someone Else How to Do It
- Email Management
- Evaluate Your Resources
- Calendar Management
- Build in a Cushion
- Put a Limit on Your Time
- Ask for Help

Strategy #1: Automation

If you find yourself doing the same thing over and over, it's time to automate. For example, you may notice that you email out the same information on a regular basis. Take a few moments to create a template, because even copying and pasting over and over again wastes time. This way you'll have it already queued up and ready to hit send.

Strategy #2: Train Someone Else How to Do It

Are you doing things you could easily teach someone else to do? Your time is too precious to spend doing work that anyone else could do with a bit of instruction. Choose several capable members of your team and train them to take over these tasks.

Strategy #3: Email Management

Do you have 1 billion emails in your inbox? Which ones do you need to keep? Decide on the threshold of number of emails in your inbox, too many versus too few. If you don't have folders created, take the time you saved by delegating your mindless tasks to archive your emails into folders. If you subscribed to lists that fill up your inbox, take a moment to unsubscribe—especially if you are always deleting them or letting them pile up unread.

Strategy #4: Evaluate Your Resources

Who around you can help you? Do you have a receptionist who has down time and can take on administrative tasks? Are there friends or family members who can lighten the load for you at home?

Strategy #5: Calendar Management

Are you using a calendar? If not, then start there. If you are using a calendar, make sure it's digital. It can be hard to let go of that good old spiral-bound organizer, but what are you going to do if you lose it? Plus, you have to haul it with you everywhere. It's time to accept that the digital age is here for good.

Big Plus: With your digital calendar—in the cloud, please—you can color-coordinate time blocks and make them repeat as needed. It will also give insight into what you've done in the past, what's coming in the future and how to visually block out your time.

Strategy #6: Build in a Cushion

When you schedule time on your digital calendar, be sure to give yourself a few extra minutes between appointments. For example, if you are scheduling appointments back-to-back-to-back, remember to give yourself time to have a bite to eat or take a short break. Perhaps you have some action items to take after each meeting. Are they going to be faint memories by your third meeting in a row? Building a time cushion may seem like it is the opposite of time-saving, but without one you are setting yourself up for more stress when things start to fall through the cracks. As a result, you risk becoming an ineffective manager.

Strategy #7: Put a Limit on Your Time

Your time is irreplaceable. What you do with it is your choice. Make sure to value both your time and that of others in meetings.

Strategy #8: Ask for Help

Managers take charge and are often extremely capable of taking on more than the average person. While this is an admirable trait, remember that someone could actually quite easily help out in a pinch. You just have to ask. Try putting a note in your digital calendar to reach out for help, and repeat this daily until it comes naturally to you.

To-Do: What other Time-Saving Strategy ideas come to mind? Did you have one that worked in the past but has since fallen by the wayside? Perhaps there are a few items on your to-do list that haven't been completed. Take a moment now to note strategies that would make your daily life easier. Don't forget to include time-saving strategies for your personal life. Your work life runs more smoothly when life at home is more organized.

Develop Your Delegation Plan

The first step in forming a customized plan is to create your very own Delegation Chart Template. Download an excel version online at *www.EmployeeManagementConsulting.com/templates*

How to Create a Delegation Chart Template

It's a good idea to create a digital chart using a spreadsheet like Excel, because it's much easier to make changes. Start by filling in the six columns in the appropriate time slot.

Column 1: Time of Day
Start from when you normally wake up until you normally go to sleep. Use increments of 15, 30 or 60 minutes, or whatever makes the most sense.

Column 2: Activity
Note the activity you typically do in each timeframe, such as walk the dog, make coffee, exercise, attend staff meeting, run reports, make sales calls or conduct client meetings. List the responsibilities you have at both home and office.

Column 3: Others Involved or Affected
Note other people who may be involved, such as kids, a spouse or partner, pets, elderly parents, co-workers, supervisors. If it is a lone activity, just put "self."

Column 4: Who Could I delegate this to?
List someone else who could do this task. Questions to ask yourself to get into the delegation mood:
- "Could an intern complete this task?"
- "Who on my staff or in my family could complete this task?"
- "Could one of my children handle this responsibly?"

Column 5: Obstacle to Delegation
Name the reason you haven't delegated this task so far, based on your fourth-column suggestions. Here are some examples of reasons:

- "It takes too much time to explain it."
- "It's easier to do it myself."
- "No one else is available or able to take it on."
- "It's something only I can do."
- "I don't trust it will be done right."

Column 6: Time Needed to Delegate
Assign the amount of time it would take you to delegate this task. For example, a few minutes, hours, over a series of weeks.

By the time you have completed the chart, you will have a good idea of the status quo. You will more than likely start to see which tasks, both at home and in the office, can be easily delegated. You will also see which tasks only you can do, as well as those that could be delegated but are riskier or will take more implementation time.

Implement Your Delegation Plan

The next step in your Delegation Plan is to implement it. First, it helps to prioritize. Look at your delegation chart and select the top three items that:

- You would most like to delegate.
- Would make the biggest impact on your life right now.

For each task, create an implementation strategy that seems realistic and comfortable for you. If you try to do it all in one day, your brain may go into overload and you will be less likely to change anything.

Then answer the following questions:

- What am I asking them to do?
- By what date do I want this delegated?
- Who will / can I delegate this to?

- When am I asking them to do it? And to complete it by when?
- How will I need to set them up for success?
- Will training be necessary? How long will that take?
- Are there others qualified to take over the training?
- How do I plan to follow up?

Your Delegation Plan is taking shape. As you begin to feel comfortable with your implementation strategy for these first three items, then you can add more to the list.

Now you are well on your way to overcoming the obstacles that have been keeping you from delegating. You have some time-saving strategies you can implement immediately, and you have a delegation plan and strategies to implement your plan. In the next chapter you will learn powerful systems that will save you time, money and stress.

Chapter 8

IT'S AS EASY AS 1, 2, 3

SYSTEMS SAVE TIME, MONEY AND STRESS: In this chapter you will learn the power of having a system—one that really works for you. When you are already overloaded, there often is no time to create a system. In this chapter, you will learn easy ways to discover and create the systems that will save you the most time and have the greatest impact on your work life. The four Strategies for Saving Time, Money and Stress are:

1. Develop an Employee Retention System
2. Work Backward
3. Uncover Obstacles
4. Create a Power Support System

Strategy #1:
Develop an Employee Retention System

When it comes to management success, employee retention is key to productivity. When it comes to your happiness, employee retention is key to your balance. Here are three systems you will need to nurture and support employee retention:

1. Communication Schedule System
2. Recognition Reminder System
3. Appreciation System

Communication Schedule System

You might be thinking, "Why would I need to schedule my communication?"

Here are some important factors to consider:
- How many employees do you manage?
- Who reports to you?
- Do you have team members off-site?
- How often do you need to communicate with your employees to make sure they feel valued and are productive?
- What type of communication is needed?
- Face-to-face?
    a. Email
    b. Phone?
    c. Staff meeting?
    d. Other?
- Do you ever need to communicate with customers?
- How do often you communicate with your supervisor?
- Do you regularly check in with other departments?

Consider these questions carefully, because the answers will help you construct a system that works best for your situation. Remember, if you call staff members into your office only when you reprimand them, they are not going to want to come into your office. That's a great example of why it's important to have a communication schedule.

5 Questions to Create an Effective Communication Schedule

1. How often do I need to communicate to my entire staff?
2. What needs to be communicated to the entire staff on a regular basis?
3. What form of communication is most appropriate to communicate to my entire staff?
4. How often do I need to deliver evaluations and to whom?

5. How can I set up communications with individual employees that will be effective and increase their productivity and sense of value?

When you have your answers, you can formulate a strategic and effective communication system. You will get the hang of it as it makes your life easier and more organized. Your employees will get used to it, too. More importantly, they will learn when it is appropriate to communicate with you and in what manner.

For example if you establish one-to-one meeting times on a weekly basis with your direct reports, they can show up with specific questions, ideas, or concerns. Or you can keep being interrupted all day long with questions, ideas or concerns from all of your direct reports.

Recognition Reminder System

Managers can be extremely targeted on their goals and responsibilities. And when you're that focused, it's easy to forget to recognize the hard work of your team. You also can forget to acknowledge someone's birthday, work anniversary or contribution on a special project. It's important to have recognition reminders in place. Remember, it's all about how to make them feel valued and be productive while saving yourself time, money and stress.

4 Questions to Develop a Recognition Reminder System

1. What types of annual days would you like to recognize?
2. What is the best way to remember to recognize these events?
3. What types of other acts would you like to recognize?
4. How would you like to recognize these achievements?

If you are unsure what milestones or occasions are important to your team members, ask for suggestions.

Appreciation System

Appreciation is slightly different from Recognition, but equally beneficial. Recognition refers to a milestone, such as an anniversary or a goal that is achieved. Appreciation can occur on a more regular basis, and can be as simple as thanking someone for helping you.

If demonstrating appreciation is such a great idea and you know how to thank and appreciate people, why is it such a forgotten act?

- You get distracted.
- You are too busy.
- You meant to, but forgot.

That's why it's important to create a conscious strategic and effective Appreciation System. Remember, the more systematic you are, the better your team will respond. They will feel more valued, and you will be happier and more relaxed!

5 Simple Acts of Appreciation

1. Coffee—just how they like it.
2. Their favorite vending machine snack.
3. A post-it note on their desk or phone with a quick personal note.
4. Email or a printout of an image that says, thank you.
5. Public acknowledgement at the next staff meeting.

You can implement some or all of these today. These Acts of Appreciation are so simple and, yet, so easy to forget.

Questions to Create an Appreciation System:

- How are you going to remember to actively appreciate your employees?
- What do you need to have in place to create a culture of appreciation?
- What types of appreciation activities would you most likely do? And when?

Answer these questions honestly, but don't get overloaded. And remember to use your Delegation skills. You don't need to take on Appreciation alone. By the way, have I mentioned how much I appreciate all the work that you have done up to this point?

Strategy #2:
Work Backward

Just like a maze you would complete when you were a kid, you can always start at the end and work backward to get to the beginning. When you are developing systems, think of the end goal first, and then figure out how you got there. This method increases the probability of your systems supporting your goals.

Use the work in a previous strategy to help get you started. For example, you explored how to develop a Communication Schedule System. If your end goal as a manager is to increase sales productivity by 20%, then every system must be created with that goal in mind. Therefore, when you develop your Communication Schedule System, you would look at it through the lens of increasing sales by 20%.

Example questions to consider:
What kinds of conversations need to happen to understand how you can create an increase in sales?

1. Do you need to increase training? Hours?
2. How are you going to share the vision with the team?
3. Who needs to be on board with the goal to make the most impact?
4. Are there any tough conversations you need to have with employees who need to improve? When and how will you conduct those conversations?
5. What type of energy level do you need to have in order to make an impact on sales?
6. Who is going to be affected by this goal, and what type of communication needs to take place with those people or departments?

It is important that you have a heightened sense of awareness when you set up these systems. Sometimes they will be long-term and more concrete. Other times they will fluctuate as your end goals change. The ability to create systems is a skill that you can use no matter where you are working or what is going on in your life.

Strategy #3:
Uncover Obstacles

All of this goal setting and talk about systems sounds like a great idea, doesn't it? I am pretty sure no one would disagree that these ideas make sense. But there are many times that you probably know exactly what to do and don't do it. A big part of the equation would be omitted if I didn't address what obstacles could get in your way of creating your systems.

When you think of your work life, there are both external and internal obstacles. You might want to brush them off or blame others for your circumstances. However, it is important to bring all obstacles to the surface so that you can face them head on.

Examples of External Obstacles:
- Lack of Support from Other Stakeholders
- Insufficient Budget
- Lack of Human Resources
- Problematic Employees
- Minimal Training

What other external obstacles do you feel are in your life? Perhaps you have a health challenge or personal obligation that has become an obstacle. I bring these up because this is real life. Things happen in your life and in the lives of your employees. I tell people, "If you are waiting for the road to be smoothly paved, you will never take the first step."

For example, if your parental responsibilities are an obstacle, you are obviously not going to get rid of your kids! But have you gotten into a pattern of feeling like you have no other options to the amount of stress you have? Here is where you can apply the other lessons we have covered. Reflect on what you've learned about delegation, asking for help, listing your resources and asking questions. Don't assume that there is no solution, because you do have choices available.

Here's an example that is office-related. Perhaps there has been a downturn in the economy and your budget has been cut significantly. Perhaps the amount of money currently available to you is out of your control. But, you still have your power of influence, your creativity and the ideas of your staff. Try not to underestimate the value of these. I have seen people barter services, have had interns or volunteers pitch in, have received donations of equipment—just to name a few possibilities. When you can open your mind to what else is possible, you give yourself the opportunity to be pleasantly surprised.

Consider your external obstacles and then look at them in a different light.

External Obstacle Exercise:

1. List your external obstacles to management success.
2. Focus on what is possible.
3. Write out additional perspectives you can create about each obstacle.

Now, take a look at the Internal Obstacles. I actually think these are the trickier ones, yet the good news is you are actually in control of your internal obstacles. Or are you?

Examples of Internal Obstacles:

- Assuming You Need to be Perfect
- Being Your Employees' Friend
- Fear of Lack of Control
- Not Trusting Your Instincts
- Being Someone You're Not
- Thinking You're Not Good Enough
- Fear of Failure / Success

This list could be a million miles long and each obstacle is unique to each person when the root cause is discovered.

The irony is that these obstacles are, in fact, in your control. You can overcome them, and they are in your hands. Then why do so many people have so many issues? Probably because they don't usually even realize that these obstacles are there in the first place. Most people do not invest the time or money to understand their internal dialogue.

In order to be an effective manager and a top-notch leader, you must invest in yourself and discover what these obstacles are for you. Find out what part of your history they are connected to and how to increase your awareness when they stop you in your tracks. Once you understand this part of yourself, you will be able to use that knowledge for the rest of your life.

That being said, the first step is discovering your internal obstacles. What thoughts do you find yourself saying? This might be something like, "I wish I could do all of this work, but I never have enough time." Or, "No matter how hard I work, I just can't seem to get ahead."

Internal Obstacle Exercise:

- List your internal obstacles to management success.
- Focus on what is possible.
- Write out additional perspectives you can create about each obstacle.

You have been digging deep in this session, and I want to ensure you have a support system to keep you on track.

Strategy #4:
Create a Power Support System

If you're anything like me, you tend to think you need to figure it all out on your own. Not true. You have lots of support, but you need to ask for it and set yourself up for success with a support system.

Imagine your ideal life as a manager:

- What systems would be in place?
- What would your daily life be like?
- How would your personal life fit into your vision?
- Who is supporting you?

Now that you have begun to formulate your vision, visit *www.EmployeeManagementConsulting.com/Templates* to download a **Power Support Template**. You can utilize this template to get you started and customize as needed. The goal is to have a career that flows, is more balanced and joyful.

You are now well on your way to creating systems that will not only save you time, money and stress, they also will help increase the balance in your work-home life. You have the tools needed to develop an Employee Retention System, an example of how working backward can be a lifesaver, an insight to your obstacles and a template to create a Power Support System.

AND, FINALLY

You are now well on your way to cultivating happy and productive employees as you complete the strategies in this book. The quicker you can implement these proven strategies, the more time you will have to focus on the big picture and develop your leadership skills.

Now is the time to shift your career trajectory and take charge of your time, increase the balance in your life and *Manage to Success*. You have a powerful position of influence. You are now prepared to lead and inspire the employees under your charge. You can make a huge impact on their lives by being a powerful mentor.

One of the most inspiring lessons I learned as a manager was how big of an impact I had on the quality of my employees' lives. They were affected by my mood, leadership skills, organizational skills, patience, ability to train, flexibility and so much more. Your employees will be affected by who you will hire, how well you train them to be successful, and your skills as a leader. Don't take your responsibility lightly.

For ongoing management training and support, join my management community of leaders at *www.EmployeeManagementConsulting.com*.

To Your Management Success,

Leisa Reid

ABOUT THE AUTHOR

Leisa Reid is a sought-after Speaker, Trainer, and Management Consultant who has presented to thousands of people throughout Southern California. After 20 years in the field of Management and Sales, Leisa founded her own company, Employee Management Consulting, where she provides profitable solutions that dramatically reduce costly employee turnover and teaches proven strategies to increase employee retention. In 2013, Leisa spearheaded and founded the OC Speakers Network, a talented group of professionals who collaborate to make their speaking and training businesses grow and thrive. More recently, she developed the "Employee Management Success System," a convenient audio training system for managers and business leaders now available on *www.EmployeeManagementConsulting.com*.

Happy AND Productive Employees? Yes! The Employee Management Success System with Leisa Reid helps you achieve both! You will learn the Step-by-Step Secrets of a Successful Manager and begin to Increase Your Free Time and Reduce Your Stress as a Manager.

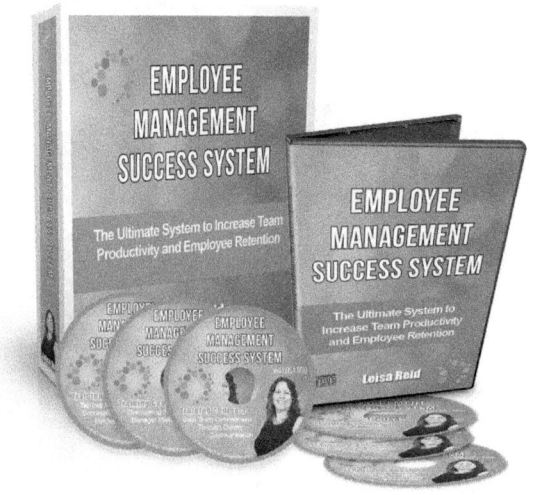

- Tap Into Your Successful Manager Mindset
- Overcoming 3 Deadly Manager Mistakes
- Gain Team Commitment Through Quality Communication
- Become a Master Delegator
- Turn Your Staff's Sense of Value into Massive Productivity
- Develop Management Systems to Save you Time, Money and Stress

Visit *www.employeemanagementconsulting.com/store* to purchase your system today!

NOTES

NOTES

NOTES

NOTES

NOTES

NOTES

NOTES

NOTES

NOTES

NOTES